A thing of beauty is a joy forever;
Its loveliness increases; it will never
Pass into nothingness.
                    JOHN KEATS, *Endymion*

R.M.S QUEEN MARY

R.M.S. Queen Mary is greeted in New York on her maiden crossing, 1936.

CUNARD LINE STATEROOM

NAME: J. BRYCE GILLESPIE
PASSENGER'S NAME IN BLOCK LETTERS
SHIP: QUEEN MARY SAILING DATE: 11-21-58
CLASS: CABIN
FROM: SOUTHAMPTON TO: NEW YORK
PORT OF EMBARKATION PORT OF LANDING

AMERICAN ADDRESS: 3425 WONDER VIEW DRIVE
LOS ANGELES, CALIF., USA

EUROPEAN ADDRESS: STRAND HOTEL
LONDON, ENGLAND

Print Deck and Room Number Here:
"B" DECK
CABIN #293

Perhaps the most famous vessel ever launched. The Super Liner *R.M.S. Queen Mary* has established her place in the hearts of millions. The proud "Queen" carried whole divisions of fighting men during World War II years. Thousands of nautical miles are now behind her as she takes up a new life. A mecca for countless thousands to marvel at in years to come. Many past travelers, including the ex-soldier showing off the "Queen" to his son, will be able to reminisce.

Photo taken in 1936. Triumphal progress down the Clyde River, Scotland. The very first voyage of the Queen Mary. Much equipment remained to be installed, including many of the lifeboats.

The Commemorative Medal issued on the Day of Launch, September 26, 1934. Depicted are his late majesty King George V and Queen Mary. The Number 534 was John Brown & Co. Yard Number.

A MARINE SAGA BEGINS

When the liner was known simply as No. 534. Picture taken during course of construction.

"Queen Mary" Fact Capsule

Horsepower—160,000
Service Speed—28.50 Knots
Fastest Average Speed—31.69 Knots
Displaces 77,500 Tons of Water
Beam (Width)—118 Feet
27 Public Rooms
2,500 Square Feet of Glass
Over 2,000 Portholes
More than 10,000,000 rivets were driven home in the "Queen's" construction.

Constantly we are intrigued to follow the pattern of one event upon another until the chain of circumstance has gone full cycle. It is fitting, therefore, since the *Queen Mary* has made her last port of call the United States, that had it not been for an American the *Queen Mary* might not have existed.

In the mid-17th century the family Cunard had emigrated from Wales to Philadelphia, a later generation moving to Nova Scotia. There, in Halifax, was born Samuel Cunard, a boy who grew up to love ships and to be consumed by a dream of harnessing steam to drive them.

Ridiculed and scorned by his fellow countrymen, in 1838 he finally sailed for Britain. In London he fared no better, but undaunted he travelled north to Scotland. In Glasgow he was introduced to two Scottish shipping men who listened attentively to this enthusiastic foreigner, and were convinced. As a result of their cooperation the Cunard Company came into being.

Two years later the *Britannia*, the first ship of Samuel Cunard's famous trans-Atlantic steam service, was launched, soon to be followed by her sister-ships the *Acadia*, *Caledonia* and *Columbia*. These fine vessels provided fortnightly sailings between Liverpool, Halifax and Boston.

How great would have been the amazement of Samuel Cunard had he realized that one day a ship would be added to the fleet he had founded, so huge that the *Britannia* could have been accommodated comfortably in one of the funnels.

In 1926 the first plans were laid to build the new liner. The task ahead would prove a difficult one. She was to be a graceful, beautiful ship, but also she had to be reliable, comfortable, and above all safe, able to withstand the most severe North Atlantic gales. Endless discussions were carried out behind closed doors. Models were built, stress tests carried out, and final acceptance of the plans was given four years later. She was to be a queen among ships, faster and larger than any previously built.

The year was 1930. Time had come for construction to begin at the famous John Brown's shipyard on the Clyde. Work surged ahead on this mammoth venture, and while the dark cloud of depression spread over the British Isles the Clydesiders were untroubled, imagining themselves to be immune from the awful penury of unemployment. But by December 1931 the Cunard Company was seriously affected, trans-Atlantic trade had fallen perilously, and on December 11th the decision was taken that work on the new liner must be suspended. Waves of shock rippled through the shipyard. A sad and lean Christmas lay ahead, with many grim, despairing days to follow.

But not only the Clydesiders mourned the abandonment of their lovely lady. Already she held a special and affectionate place in the hearts of all the people, so much that Cunard was inundated with offers of help. Alas! without tremendous financial resources she could not be saved, and so she lay forlorn and forsaken for twenty-eight lonely months.

In March 1934 the Government finally voted Cunard a grant of nine and a half million pounds sterling, and a week later work began once more.

One can imagine the scene on that first morning . . . the shipyard gates thrown wide . . . the workers eagerly streaming in . . . marching in time to the pipeband. To any Scot, at any time, the skirl of the pipes must tug at the heartstrings. How moving then, on such a day, with all Clydebank turned out to watch. The harsh days of deprivation were over. There was much rejoicing and thanksgiving on the Clyde.

Six months later she was ready to take to the water, and it was fitting that since she was to be launched by the Queen, she should be named the *Queen Mary.*

It would be well to refute here the oft-repeated rumour that the ship was named the *Queen Mary* due to a misunderstanding on the part of H.M. King George V. The story goes that Cunard had intended to name the new ship the "Queen Victoria" following their tradition of having the
CONTINUED

Over 4000 craftsmen worked on the Queen Mary. *Men file off after shift in John Brown's shipbuilding yard in Scotland.*

"Queen Mary"

Miniature waves enabled the design team to evaluate the liner's behavior in various seas.

Fitting one of the four 35 ton propellers, the cone shaped cap will be placed into position.

One of the turbine rotors. Each of the 64,166 blades is hand set.

Tugs take charge directly after launch. At this stage the "Queen" was a shell, waiting on tons of machinery to fill her cavernous interior.

names of their ships end in "ia" as in the Britannia, Lusitania, Mauretania, Aquitania, etc. During his visit to Scotland, a director of Cunard was asked by the King how the new ship progressed. The director advised that progress was very satisfactory and that the Company hoped for permission to name her "after the most illustrious woman who has ever sat on the English throne." The king, supposing this to be a compliment to his wife, was deeply touched and answered, "I shall ask Queen Mary's permission".

This story is completely untrue and without foundation.

There was a simple explanation for this seeming deviation in names. Cunard Company and Oceanic Company had recently merged to become Cunard White Star Limited. There had to be a name acceptable to both. What better than the *Queen Mary?*

September 26, 1934, was a cold, wet, miserable day, but it would have taken more than typical Scottish weather to dampen the spirits of the estimated two hundred and fifty thousand men, women and children who had gathered to watch their sovereign launch her namesake and wish her God-speed.

Amidst triumphant siren blasts of tugboats and the tremendous cheering roar of the spectators, and with a mightly clanging of chains, slowly, hesitantly, then quickly gathering speed the pride of the John Brown Yard imposingly slipped down the launching ways until her stern hit the water, causing a tremendous wave that lapped over the river banks to the adjacent fields. The Queen of the Seas was safely afloat!

In his speech at the launching ceremony King George said, "Samuel Cunard built his ships to carry the mails between the two English-speaking countries. This one is built to carry the people of the two lands in great number to and fro so that they may learn to understand each other . . . Both are faced with similar problems, and prosper and suffer together.

. . . "May her life among great waters spread friendship among the nations."

These were to prove prophetic words.

But she was still only a shell. For a further eighteen months in the fitting-out basin the prodigious job of installing machinery, equipment and furnishings went on. At times a nightmare task, but exciting and fulfilling nonetheless, as her character took shape and she was transformed from an empty hulk to a luxurious hotel.

When it was known that she was ready to leave the Clyde the people came by the thousands to give her a send-off, many camping out all night. By morning a million people thronged the river banks. Her great booming siren can carry ten miles across the ocean and yet is so deep and mellow that one can stand

CONTINUED

Waiting on the ways for the release mechanism to let her slide into the River Clyde. A ship of this magnitude takes over a year to complete after launch in a fitting out basin.

Picture taken in fitting out basin just after the launch. Note graceful sheer of her proud bow.

Mermaid cocktail bar, a cabin class rendezvous.

The public rooms were noted for their lavish use of exotic woods.

Dining was always a delightful experience aboard ship.

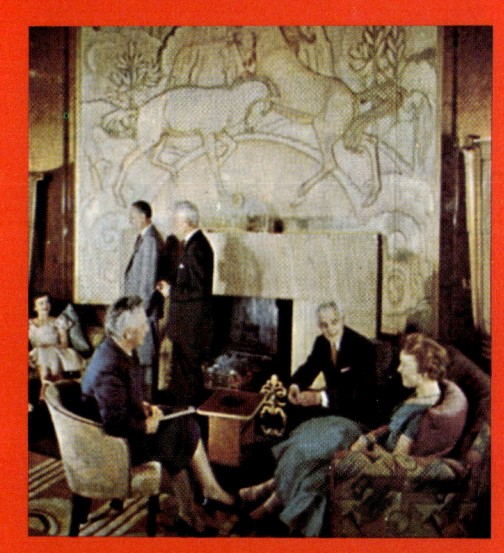

Section of the main lounge, with its famous mural.

From Raw Steel to the Ultimate in Elegance

CONTINUED

quite close and not be deafened. Now, for the first time, it rent the air in salute as she moved slowly out into the main stream. After five years she was starting out on her career, an illustrious career that would justify the faith of all who loved her.

The towering side of the great ship, taken in the fitting-out basin. Note scaffolding around bridge superstructure. Lifeboat is being used in test of davits.

cheering wildly. It was such a welcome as perhaps only New York can stage.

Good-bye and God bless you and all who sail in you, on this fair March morning.

At Southhampton, huge drydocking facilities had been specifically built, and it was there that she went to be thoroughly checked and to have the special propellers fitted for her speed trials. All went well.

On May 28, 1936, Queen Mary's birthday, the "Mary," as she was to be affectionately known, was being nudged away from the quay, eased out of her berth. What a send-off she received. Intermingled were the roaring of thousands of spectators, the shrill whistles of the small craft filling Southampton Water, the deafening noise of planes circling and diving overhead, the bands playing "Rule Britannia," and the cheering passengers crowding the decks. Royally, the *Queen Mary* headed for the Channel. Her maiden voyage had begun.

A tumultuous welcome awaited her when she approached New York. Flowers were dropped by circling airplanes, a veritable fleet of flag-bedecked small boats, in the wake of the famous fire-boats, filled the air with their cacophony of hoots, toots and whistles. The happy crowds lined the banks of the river,

The *Queen Mary* had broken no records on her maiden voyage. She had crossed the Atlantic in 4 days, 5 hours, 46 minutes at an average speed of 29.13 knots. She was 42 minutes behind the record achieved by the *Normandie*.

While Cunard policy has always been that competition is at variance with safety, nevertheless they would be the first to admit that if a ship holds the coveted Blue Riband her worth is increased immeasurably.

The most famous of the ocean race tracks is that from Bishop's Rock to the Ambrose Light. Bishop's Rock lighthouse is off the Scilly Isles, almost 200 miles west of Southampton. The Ambrose Lightship is moored in New York Bay.

In August of that year great crowds of people awaited the

arrival of the *Queen Mary* at Southampton. She had brought the Blue Riband to Britain, having reached Ambrose Light in 4 days, 27 minutes at an average speed of 30.14 knots, despite head winds and fog during the latter part of her voyage. On her return she triumphantly passed Bishop's Rock 3 days, 23 hours, 57 minutes after leaving Ambrose Light, at an average speed of 30.63 knots. Her Company and all Britain were justifiably proud of her magnificent achievement.

Until 1937 the *"Mary"* held the record, when the *Normandie* recaptured it on a westbound voyage of 3 days, 23 hours, 36 minutes, and a return voyage of 3 days, 22 hours, 7 minutes at 31.2 knots. However, in August 1938 the *Queen Mary* regained

CONTINUED

The proud lion emblem of Cunard Lines.

Attention to detail was synonymous with the name *Queen Mary*. Here the ship's bellboys line up for daily inspection. Their requirements were: intelligence, neatness, a desire to oblige, quickness and a keen love of sea service. With the "Queen's" 12 decks, 6 miles of carpeted space and 21 elevators, it was a demanding world for these eager lads.

the record with an incredible westbound voyage of 3 days, 21 hours, 48 minutes and eastbound return in 3 days, 20 hours, 42 minutes at an average speed of 31.69 knots. This record she held until 1952 when our *United States* captured the Blue Riband, crossing the Atlantic at 34 knots!

When war was declared in London on 3rd September, 1939, the *Queen Mary* was sailing westbound for New York. She remained in New York until March of the following year, when she was conscripted by the British Government. Camouflaged with dull gray paint she sailed for Australia where she was converted to a troop-ship.

The *Queen Mary's* first voyage in her new role was to England, via the Cape. From there she ferried desperately-needed troops to the Middle East, thereafter shuttling troops between Australia and the Middle East. After the United States entered

The "Queen!"

Sailing for an "unknown" destination in 1940, painted in wartime gray. The Hudson River was a familiar haven to the "Mary" during W.W. II.

Peacetime saw the "Queen" making 1001 roundtrips between Southampton, Cherbourg and Manhattan.

The *Queen Mary* was out of service twice during each year. 10 day drydocking and refurnishing in summer and a six-week refit in winter.

During her express days in the Atlantic, 48 hours was her home port time, only 24 hours at New York.

The *"Mary"* boasted 12,000 varied types of plants and had a gardener-at-sea to care for them!

Rare photograph showing the three largest liners at start of W.W. II. Ill-fated Normandie on left, Queen Mary center, Queen Elizabeth getting up steam on right.

The shopping arcade offered duty free items.

the war she transported American servicemen from New York to Australia, and from New York to the United Kingdom.

The *Queen Mary* and her sister-ship, the *Queen Elizabeth,* were outfitted to carry a record number of soldiers. Each was capable of lifting 15,000 men (an entire division) at a time, and between them they carried thousands of the 865,000 American troops sent to Britain during the war years. On her return voyages she frequently carried Italian and German prisoners-of-war, bound for Canada.

Being equipped with radar proved to be invaluable, for the *Queen Mary* never sailed in convoy and was only intermittently escorted, since her speed made a torpedo attack by a German U-boat almost impossible. Also, because of her speed and size, she was difficult to escort, and this resulted in her involvement in an exceedingly tragic accident in 1942.

The *Queen Mary* was transporting to the U. K. another division of GI's. As she approached the Clyde she came under the escort and protection of HMS *Curacao,* a cruiser of 5000 tons. U-boats were known to be in the vicinity and both ships followed the usual, prearranged pattern of a zigzag course. But somehow there was a miscalculation in timing, and in seconds the 80,000 ton *Queen Mary* had sliced the cruiser in half. The naval ship sank immediately. Apart from a crumpled bow the *Queen Mary* suffered no damage, but over 300 men of the Royal Navy were lost on HMS *Curacao*. Rigid regulations forbade the *Queen Mary* to stop, for by so doing she would have endangered all the men she was carrying and so she could only summon help and limp sadly home. The destroyers HMS *Bramham* and HMS *Cowdray* raced to the scene to pick up survivors, of which there were only one hundred.

She was a prize coveted by Hitler, naturally. Indeed whoever could sink the *Queen Mary* had been promised the Iron Cross with oak leaves, promotion and glory, but she was destined to survive the war years.

CONTINUED

The Might of the "Queen!"

Who wouldn't seize the chance of a tour of this ship's power plant?— the mightiest assembly of machinery ever put into a liner. Deep down, at the bottom of the "Queen," 40 feet below the waterline, the engineers' shift of more than 100 officers and men watched over the powerful engines that propelled the *R.M.S. Queen Mary.* The three shift working staff numbered 350! An express elevator whisked the men through eight decks, to the maze of pipes, valves and boilers.

We will try to explain the workings of this mass of equipment. The basic design is four screws, driven by steam turbines. While there is an auxiliary boiler room with 3 watertube boilers, there are four main boiler-rooms, each containing six watertube boilers. These consist of a huge cluster of steel tubes into which water is pumped. White hot flames superheat these tubes. Each boiler had 7 burners. 1¾ tons of oil was burned every hour, 42 tons on a 24-hour shift, 1,008 tons for all the main twenty-four high pressure boilers. A total of 3½ million gallons of converted sea water was turned into steam every day. To burn this quantity of fuel needs air, prodigious amounts, 20,000 tons each day. 32 huge fans were continuously at work. This is the reason for the large ventilators you can see on the upper deck. The boiler-rooms were air tight, so the air is blown into the furnaces, not just drawn in. Hence, the word "forced draught." It is a complex system to superheat steam to 720 degrees for the high pressure turbines. The steam passes through four sets of turbines. These are coupled to the four huge drive shafts. Reduction gearing turns the turbine shafts to 180 revolutions per minute. Picture the huge 35 ton propellers whirling at 3 turns every second! This is fantastic power. It would have to be. The "Queen" could race into Atlantic seas doing over 30 miles per hour, all 81,000 tons of her!

CROSS SECTION OF

Builder's plate

The "Queen" was driven by single reduction geared turbines. Four screw propellers, each being driven by an independent set of machinery. Each set comprising a large gear wheel. This in turn connected to the line shafting. Actuated through pinions by the four turbines working in series. Astern turbines incorporated in the casings of two "ahead" turbines. Each set of engines had independent condensing plants. These consisted of large surface condenser with circulating and condensate pumps. There were two separate main engine rooms. Two engines in each. Two auxiliary engine rooms housed turbo generators and all types of auxiliary machinery.

THE MAIN ENGINES

Q. M. GOES TO WAR

During her troop carrying days, the "Mary" could make her port turnaround in 4 days. This was an incredible feat in those war years. 15,000 service personnel were all off in just over 36 hours. Then provisions and more V.I.P. passengers and large contingents of prisoners were loaded in Britain. To control this load of people, the vessel was divided into 3 major sections, each with its distinctive color. Upon entering, the G.I.'s were given metal tags, corresponding to their appointed area. M.P.'s checked to make sure rules were kept. Two meals were served, breakfast and dinner. It took six separate sittings to complete one feeding. Chow line began at 6:30 a.m. and went on 'til evening. Over 400 tons of food was consumed each round trip. Just one item, eggs, 30,000 a voyage cooked. One way traffic was in effect. Starboard passageways/forward going personnel. Port for aft moving traffic. Troop loading would start at 9 p.m. with ferries, etc. moving back and forth from the Jersey side of the river. Dawn would see the last soldiers aboard and the *Queen Mary* would slip out to face the perils of fog, heavy seas and prowling subs.

The "Queen" slices through the sea, packed with G.I.'s on their way to Britain.

CONTINUED

For the return of the first of her G.I.'s New York had laid on a fantastic welcome. The war in Europe was over, the victorious boys were home. The great liner, flags flying, sailed majestically into the harbour to an overwhelming reception, a tribute not only to her soldiers but also a tribute to the "Mary." For Churchill has said that the service rendered by her undoubtedly shortened the duration of the war.

A return to peace and yet again alterations were being made to the *Queen Mary*. She had started her career as a trans-Atlantic liner, had been converted to a troopship, had served as a hospital ship, and now she was to be known as the "Brides" ship. She was to carry thousands of British girls to be reunited with the servicemen they had married during the war years.

During her years of war service she had carried over 800,000 passengers, and had covered half a million miles. Now the gigantic task of refurbishing her was to begin. Once more she would sail as a luxury passenger liner.

During her long and honorable career the "Mary" had carried many illustrious passengers, many world famous personalities, many unassuming passengers. All held her in deep affection and respect. In fact, many turned the final voyage, from England via Cape Horn into a sea-going pilgrimage.

Now her last voyage is over. She lies quietly, graciously, at her special berth in Long Beach, her former glory undiminished.

We salute a great lady. GOD BLESS THE QUEEN!

The rudder has inspection door for easy access.

Largest rudder on any liner — 65 tons

Dramatic stern view gives idea of the "Queen's" grandeur.

On March 21, 1940, newly painted gray, the *Queen Mary* slipped down the Hudson River to begin her career as a troop carrier. Cape Town was her first port, on leaving New York. After bunkering, she set course for Sydney, Australia. Here she was stripped of her plush interior fittings. In only 14 days she was transformed into a troopship. Used early in the war, she bolstered Monty's forces in the Middle East. Most of '41 saw her based in Sydney, ferrying troops to Alexandria.

In 1942, during a stay in New York, her capacity was increased once again. This time an entire division could be accommodated. During 1942 the *Queen Mary* had a narrow escape. She was in harbor at Rio, to take on fuel. With some real cloak and dagger work, it was discovered that a Nazi clique were about to wireless a U-boat pack. They were lying in wait for their most prized target! Fortunately, the "Queen" changed her course plans and managed to elude the enemy submarines.

The liner helped to crush Rommel during the battle of El Alamein. Her role was vital in bringing in badly needed reinforcements, at a very crucial period. In 1943 the *Queen Mary* made her last journey to the Mediterranean and "Aussie" waters. This voyage covered more than 40,000 nautical miles. Towards the middle of '43 saw the "Mary" making her famous series of shuttle runs from the East Coast to British Ports. Soon it was American soldiers sailing over and Italian/German prisoners traveling back to internment.

The *Queen Mary* was protected with special de-gaussing heavy copper strips sheathed in rubber girdles. Oerlikon and rocket firing guns were manned by Naval gun crews.

The initial D-Day invasion plans were formulated on board the Q.M. crossing to Halifax in August, 1943. Churchill wrote, "The Q.M. drove on through the waves and we lived in comfort on board. As usual on these voyages, we worked all day long (200 staff, plus 50 Marine guards). Our large cipher staff, with attendant cruisers to dispatch outgoing messages, kept us in touch from hour to hour. Each day I studied with the Chiefs of Staff the various aspects of the problems we were to discuss with our American friends, the most important of these, was, of course, 'Overlord.'"

The Prime Minister's name on the secret passenger list was "Colonel Warden," Churchill's wartime pseudonym. In the first-class suites the great task of preparing for D-Day went on into the wee hours, while the great ship's prow forced the seas apart on her evasive course, making wide sweeps to port and starboard. (This was antisubmarine strategy imperative for such a momentous journey.)

Churchill's final round-trip voyage took place in 1944. This was for the second Quebec conference in September.

CONTINUED

THE STEERING MECHANISM

The mighty rudder of the Queen Mary weighs 65 tons. It is moved by an electro-hydraulic system, as shown here. One touch of the steering wheel on the bridge controls a valve and from this small pipes run nearly three-quarters of the length of the ship to the steering department. By small electrically operated hydraulic cylinders the pressure is raised and transmitted to another set of cylinders, where again it is raised and passed to the final servo-motor stage. Here powerfully driven pumps force oil into large hydraulic cylinders and work rams in or out as required. The rams are attached to the tiller of the rudder which they move backwards and forwards, and these move the rudder to and fro, and the whole system is duplicated with two wheels on the bridge, either of which can be used instantly to bring about the same result. There is also a hand-controlled motor in the steering-room for emergencies. The wash from the propellers acts on the rudder and turns the ship.

THE QUEEN SIZE SIRENS

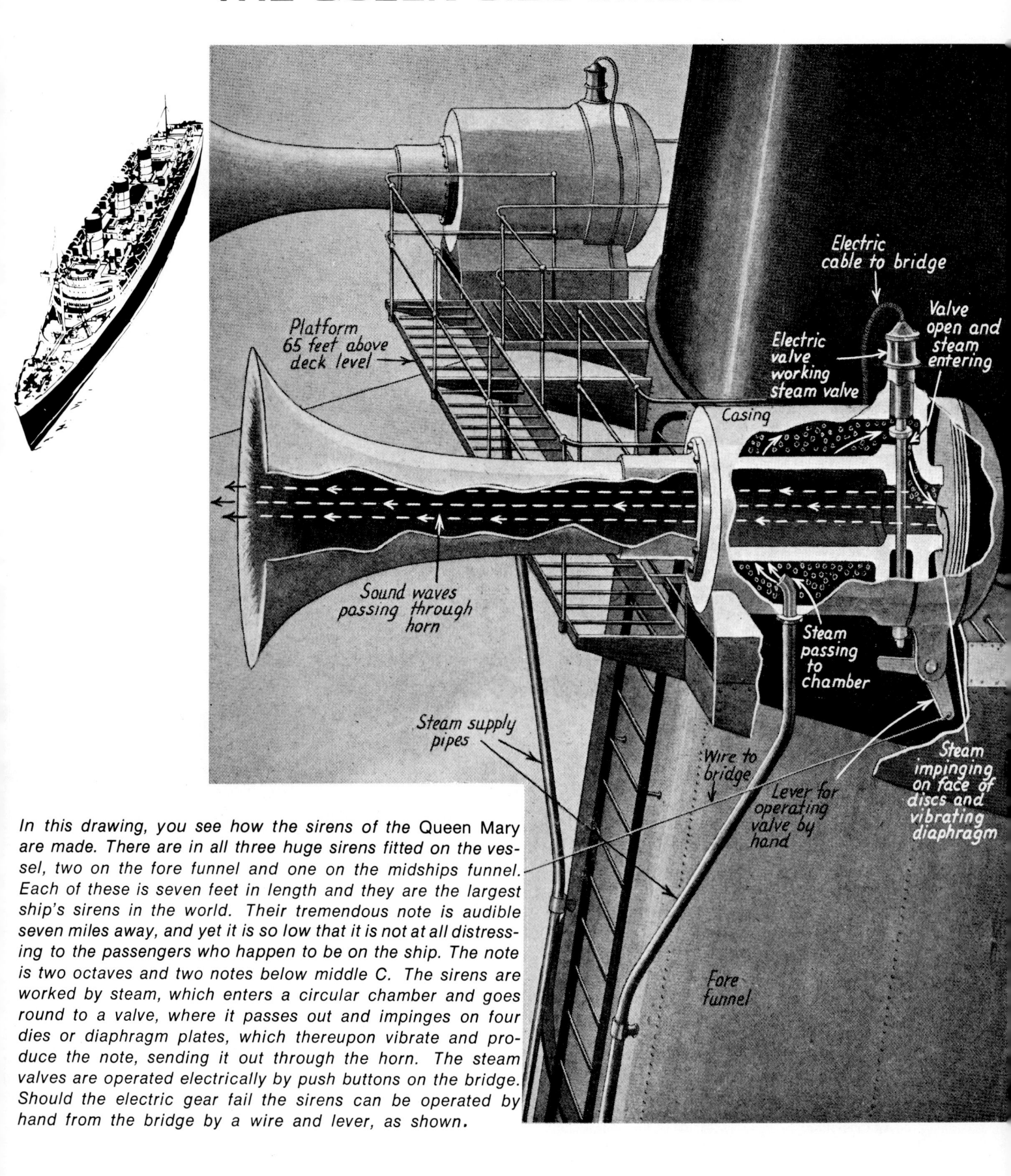

In this drawing, you see how the sirens of the Queen Mary are made. There are in all three huge sirens fitted on the vessel, two on the fore funnel and one on the midships funnel. Each of these is seven feet in length and they are the largest ship's sirens in the world. Their tremendous note is audible seven miles away, and yet it is so low that it is not at all distressing to the passengers who happen to be on the ship. The note is two octaves and two notes below middle C. The sirens are worked by steam, which enters a circular chamber and goes round to a valve, where it passes out and impinges on four dies or diaphragm plates, which thereupon vibrate and produce the note, sending it out through the horn. The steam valves are operated electrically by push buttons on the bridge. Should the electric gear fail the sirens can be operated by hand from the bridge by a wire and lever, as shown.

GROSS TONNAGE:

Queen Mary	81,237
Queen Elizabeth	83,673
Norway (formerly the France)	70,202
USS New Jersey	56,000
Titanic	46,328
Royal Viking Star	29,000
Pacific Princess	20,000

QUEEN MARY SHIPWALK ROUTE

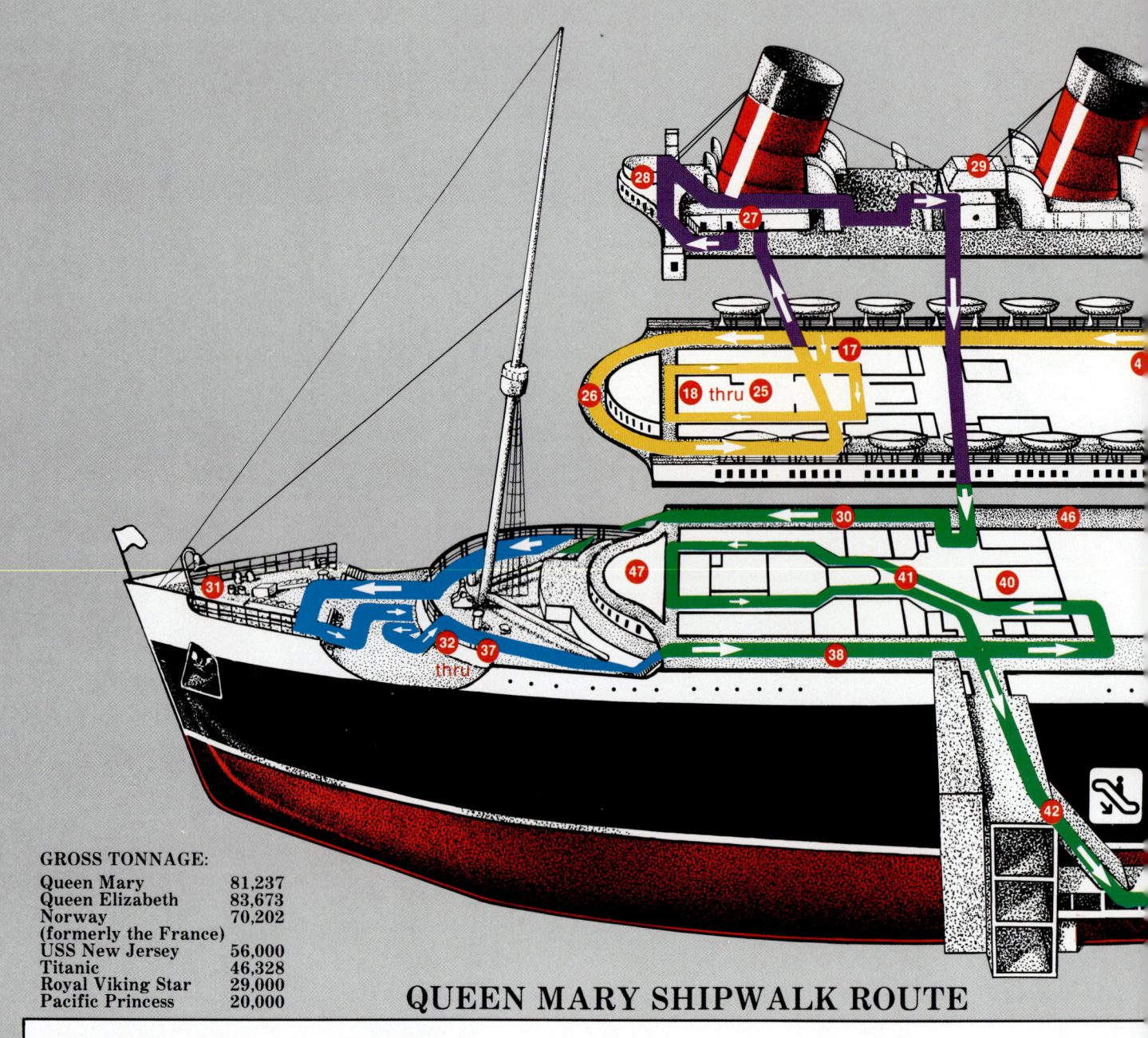

1. Entrance to Lower Decks Shipwalk
2. First Class Starboard Gallery
3. Queen Mary Printing Presses
4. Queen Mary Story—an Audio Visual Presentation
5. Anchor and Whistle
6. Engine Room—a Sound and Light Presentation
7. Shaft Alley
8. Emergency Steering Station
9. Propeller
10. Master Model Builder Workshop
11. The Royal Theater Dreyer's Puppet Show
12. Hall of Maritime Heritage
13. Escalator to Upper Decks
14. Aft Observation Point
15. 40MM Anti-Aircraft Gun
16. Lifeboat Display and Demonstration
17. Sun Deck Exhibits Entrance
18. Gymnasium
19. First Class Children's Playroom
20. First Class Drawing Room
21. Dining Table Settings
22. World War II Displays
23. Chapel
24. Hospital
25. Barber Shop
26. Bow Observation Point
27. Officer's Quarters
28. Bridge and Wheelhouse—Entrance to Sound and Light Presentation
29. Wireless Radio Room
30. Promenade Deck Starboard
31. Ship's Bow
32. Entrance to Bow Exhibits
33. Cabin and Tourist Class Staterooms
34. First Class Suite and Maid Quarters
35. Long Gallery/First Class Sitting Room
36. Purser's Desk
37. Fire Station
38. Promenade Deck Port
39. Queen's Salon
40. Passenger Information
41. Piccadi[lly]
42. Escalat[or to] London [...] Parking
43. Veranda[h]
44. Sir Win[ston] Restaur[ant]
45. Sun Dec[k]
46. Promen[ade]
47. Observa[tion]

NOT O[N...]

LOWER DECKS

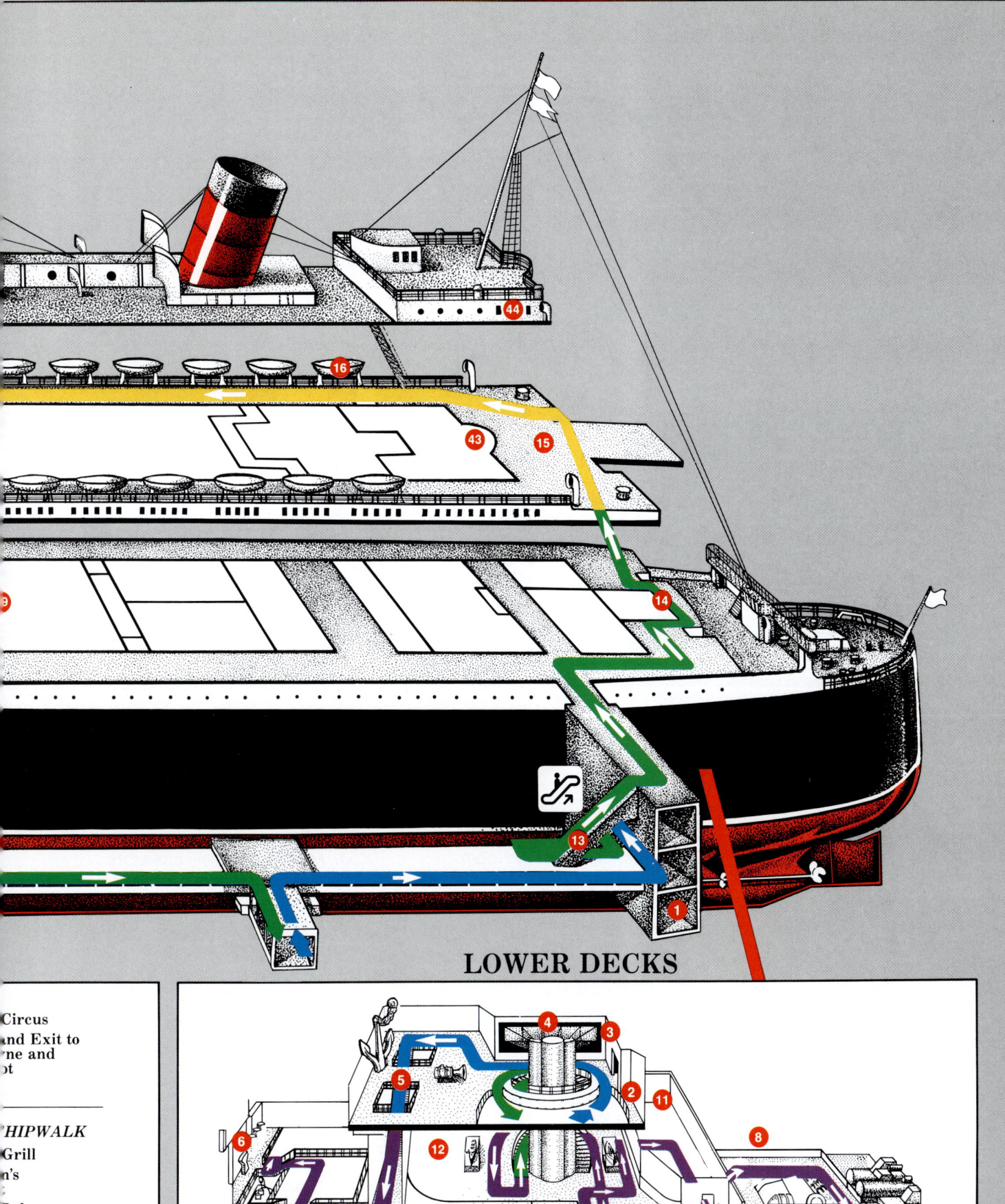

Circus
and Exit to
~~~ne and
~~t

~~~HIPWALK
Grill
~~'s
Bakery
e Cafe
n Bar

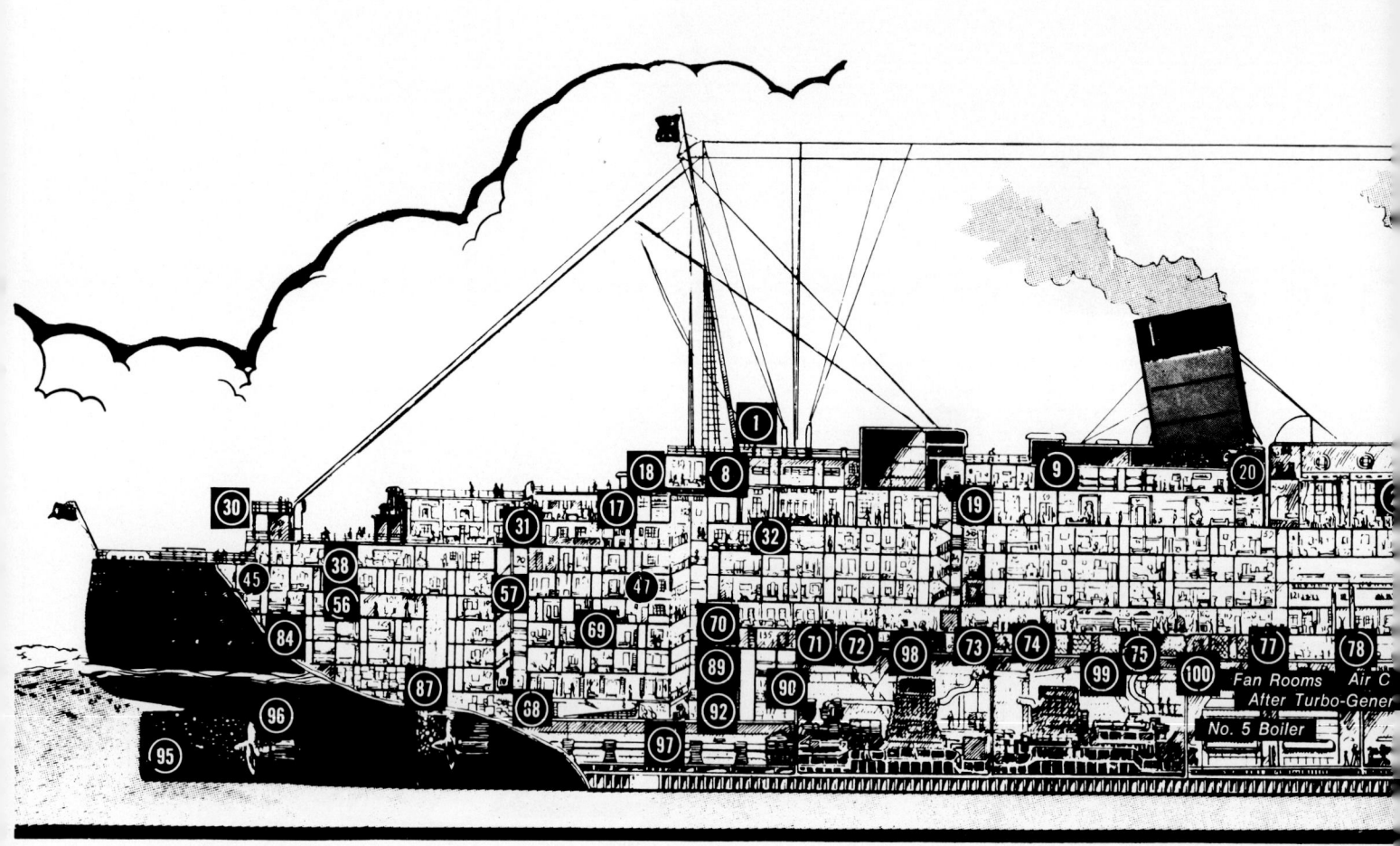

CROSS-SECTION DIAGRA

SPORTS DECK
1. Main Mast
2. Sports Deck
3. Navigation—Radar
4. Searchlights
5. Chart Room
6. Wheelhouse—Bridge
7. Captain—Officer Quarters

SUN DECK
8. Verandah Grill
9. Engineering Officers
10. Cinema
11. Gymnasium
12. Squash Racquet Court
13. Wireless Room
14. Luxury Suites
15. Forward Staircase
16. Elevators

PROMENADE DECK
17. Tourist Smoking Room
18. Pantry
19. Ballroom
20. Starboard Gallery
21. Lounge Stage
22. Main Lounge
23. Writing Rooms
24. Main Hall & Shopping Center
25. Drawing Room
26. Altar
27. Children's Playroom
28. Cocktail & Observation Lounge
29. Promenade

MAIN DECK
30. Docking Bridge
31. Tourist Lounge

32. Writing Room & Library
33. Main Staircase—Elevators
34. Garden Lounge
35. Cargo Hatch
36. Foremast
37. Crow's Nest

"A" DECK
38. "A" Deck Lounge
39. Suites & Bedrooms
40. Purser's Office
41. Tourist Class Beauty Shop
42. Fore Hatch
43. Rope Locker
44. Forecastle

"B" DECK
45. Crew's Quarters
46. Suites & Bedrooms
47. Hairdresser's

M OF THE QUEEN MARY

"C" DECK
55. Crew Area
56. Stern Capstan Room
57. Staircase & Elevators
58. Tourist Dining Salon
59. Bake Shop
60. Vegetable Room
61. Kitchens
62. The Grill Room
63. China Pantry
64. Cocktail Bar
65. Private Dining Room
66. Restaurant
67. Foyer

"D" DECK
68. Crew Quarters
69. Suites & Bedrooms
70. Ale & Stout Room

71. Dairy Produce
72. Fruit Stores
73. Fresh & Frozen Fish
74. Butcher Shop
75. Poultry, Game, Etc.
77. Ship's Hospital
78. Dispensary
79. Printing Shop
80. Oil Filling Station
81. Pool Dressing Room
82. Swimming Pool
83. Kosher Kitchen

"E" DECK
84. Crew Area
85. Bedrooms
86. Mail Room

"F" DECK
87. Baggage Room
88. Tourist Pool
89. Beer Stores
90. Wine Storage
91. Garage

"G" DECK
92. Linen Stores
93. Baggage Section
94. Mail Space

MACHINERY & HOLD
95. Rudder
96. Propellers
97. Shaft, Shaft Tunnels
98. After Engine Rooms
99. Forward Engine Rooms

SOME FACTS

Three acres of recreation deck space equal to a large football stadium.

The main foyer measures 111 feet by 70 feet. It contains smart shopping center, with book shop, phone booths, haberdashery and boutiques.

Six special oil filling stations allowed the Queen Mary to be fueled in just under eight hours

Main restaurant is perhaps the largest room ever built into a liner. It contains 16,874 square feet, accommodating 768 passengers at one sitting. Steel hull plates range in length from 30 feet down to eight.

The three vessels that crossed to the New World with Columbus could fit into the main foyer of the *Queen Mary*.

The main engines could generate a total of 160,000 horse power. This is equal to the pulling power of forty large locomotives.

The total weight of steel in the hull and machinery exceeded 50,000 tons.

It would take forty miles of freight cars to carry the "Mary's" weight.

10,000,000 rivets would equal a pyramid of 25,000 cubic ft.

65 Pullman Sleepers would be needed to move the 2200 passengers which the "Mary" could carry on one Transatlantic crossing

The 200 People that were Passengers & Crew on the First Cunarder, Britannia.

The "Queen's" refrigeration complex would meet the needs of 15,000 tract homes.

Scale drawing showing the enormity of her anchors.

Her anchors are equal in weight to twenty automobiles. Each link in her cable chain is two ft. Each of her two anchors carried 990 ft. of chain.

Over half a million pieces of glassware, china and table silver were used on "The Queen." 21,000 table cloths, 30,000 bedsheets, 210,000 towels, were just part of the ship's inventory.

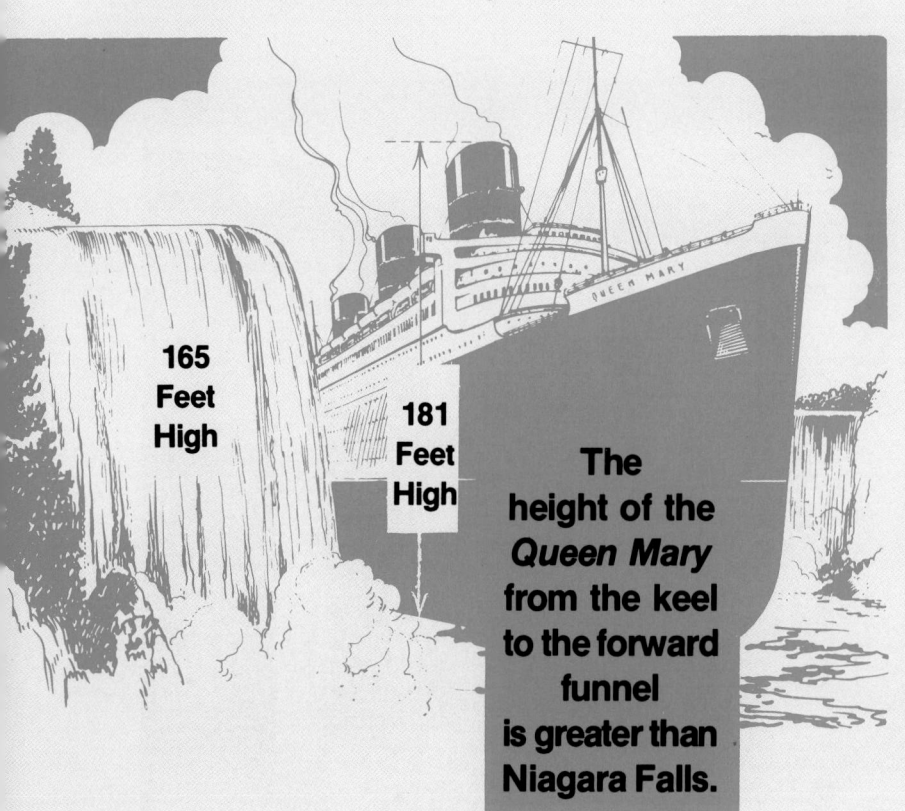

165 Feet High

181 Feet High

The height of the *Queen Mary* from the keel to the forward funnel is greater than Niagara Falls.

FACT CAPSULE

The "Queen" wrested the famous Blue Riband away from the French Liner "Normandie" at an average speed of 31.69 knots.

The four geared turbines had a combined total of 256,664 finely adjusted blades.

The four manganese bronze propellers weighed a total of 140 tons.

Sixteen separate models were made of No. 534, these being extensively tank tested before the actual building commenced.

Over 7,000 ship model tests were carried out before the final form of this magnificent liner was determined. Simulated Atlantic weather with huge waves was all part of the rigid model tank tests.

It takes thirty tons of paint to cover her million-square feet of exterior.

Queen Mary's forward funnel is seventy feet high. This size will permit three locomotives, line abreast to fit with ample room.

View showing the main deck, with its miles of steel plating.

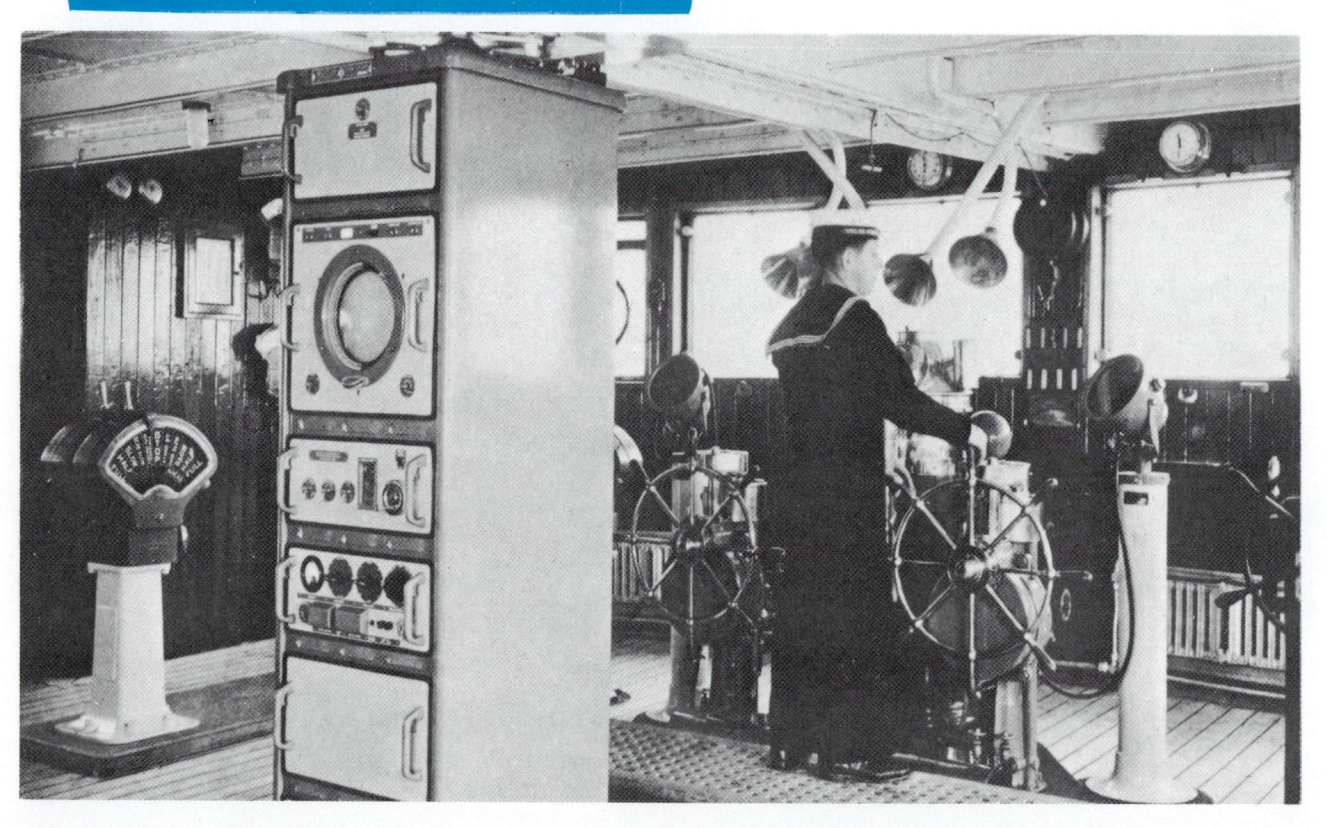

The wheelhouse with its fascinating array of steering and navigation equipment. Radar system in foreground.

The "Queen" begins to take shape. Scene shows hull being fabricated on the ways. Photo taken directly across the River Clyde. Note the Clydesdale horses working in foreground.

The original souvenir program sold on Launch Day, 1934.

HIGHLIGHTS

Adolf Hitler had a standing offer . . . $250,000 to any U-Boat crew that could sink her.

Painting the "Mary" is equal to doing over 600 private homes.

The Queen Mary weighs over one hundred million pounds.

Sir Winston Churchill crossed the Atlantic three times during the war with his operations staff.

In Long Beach, 320 tons of paint were removed (making her rise one inch and a half) before 8 tons of fresh paint were applied.

The "Queen" carried a record number of passengers (2,332) in August 1939. These were mostly U.S. citizens hurrying home, leaving Europe as W.W. II threatened.

The "Queen" had the distinction of having one of the first installations of marine radar in 1942.

The North River in New York is the locale. The "Mary" proceeds to her berth at West 50th Street, while the "United States" is being warped into her slip at West 44th Street.

Painting below has the queenly sisters passing in mid-Atlantic. Famed marine artist Charles Evers catches the feel of this happy voyage highlight, which was quite common in the fifties and sixties.

This was all part of the good life when the "Queen" offered the finest way of travel.

Dancing in the delightful Verandah Grill.

GROSS TONNAGE 81,237
DISPLACEMENT 77,500
WATER LINE LENGTH . . . . 1,004 ft.
OVER-ALL LENGTH . . . . 1,019.5 ft.
EXTREME BEAM (WIDTH) . . . . 118 ft.
KEEL TO MASTHEAD . . . . 237 ft.
KEEL TO FORWARD FUNNEL . . . . 181 ft.
TOP SUPERSTRUCTURE TO KEEL . . . . 124 ft.

Captain Treasure Jones speaks at arrival gala.

Each of *Queen Mary's* bronze propellers tip the scales at 35 tons. Tip to center measures 9 feet.

Thornycroft control panel in engineroom.

Each of the four blades are so delicately balanced, a man can turn with his hands.

Cutting through calm seas after leaving Rio.

The forward funnel is 70.5 ft. in height, from the sun deck. This is a foot higher than Central Park's Egyptian obelisk. The diameter of each funnel is 30 ft. This would permit three locomotives to pass through. Drawing shows the ancient "Britannia," Cunard Lines first passenger ship.

Flotilla of pleasure craft meet the elegant lady on her arrival day.

CUNARD

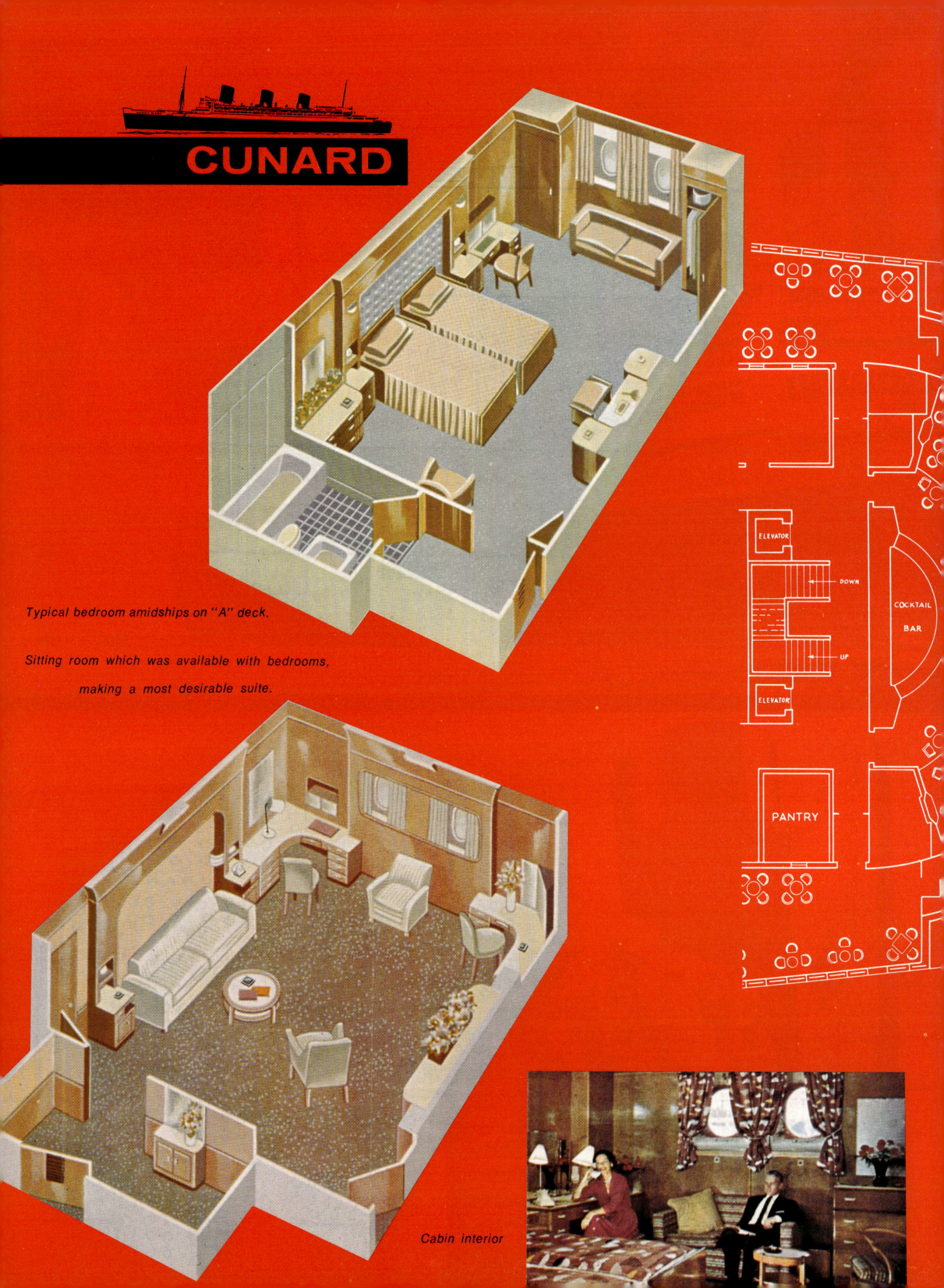

Typical bedroom amidships on "A" deck.

Sitting room which was available with bedrooms, making a most desirable suite.

Cabin interior

The tourist class smoking room.

OPEN PROMENADE

Card room and library.

The cabin class smoking room.

SOME CAREER HIGHLIGHTS

Long Beach Naval Dockyard was able to drydock the "Mary" in 1967, when she arrived from final voyage around the Horn.

Crew had their own pub, "The Pig 'N Whistle."

Including trooping duties, the "Mary" has carried over three million passengers.

Staff included 73 females.

There are 110 steps up to the crows nest. Carpeting: 10 miles / Clocks: 700 / Phones: 600 / Fastest crossing Westbound: August 1938, 3,097 nautical miles, average speed: 30.94 / Eastbound: Also August 1938, 3,128 miles, average 31.69 knots / Steamed 569,943 nautical miles in war service / *Queen Mary's* role has been that of Bride's Ship, Transatlantic Liner, Prison Ship, Cruise Ship, Hospital Ship and Troop Carrier.

At one point during WW II, the German pocket battleship "Leutzow" was loose in the Atlantic. Her specific instructions: Find the *Queen Mary*, and sink her.

In the post war years the "Mary" was the scene of many wild parties. Many times she sailed from N. Y. before all visitors had gone ashore. In such cases the "Stowaways" were put ashore by launch or pilot boat. Before 1948 (when Cunard changed their policy) as many as 12,000 visitors would crowd aboard to wish Bon Voyage to 2,000 passengers. There was a cry of resentment when passes were issued to only 2 guests per bonafide traveler.

On at least two occasions the *Queen Mary* docked in New York without the aid of her usual eight tugs. These feats of seamanship are legend with the thousands who watched.

One of the *Queen Mary's* rescues was done in a howling gale. She' raced 323 miles to the Panamanian "Liberator", which desperately needed a doctor. It was a scene of drama. Pitch black night with the searchlights playing on a volunteer lifeboat attempting to cross with the liner's surgeon. Finally success, then the even more difficult return, with two badly injured.

With passengers lining the rails, spellbound, Captain Sorrell maneuvered to give some protection in the near hurricane winds. Finally on the sixth try the small boat made it. Passengers collected a large sum, and gave it to the lifeboat's crew for their gallant work.

At one time during stringent rationing in England, the "Queen" was known as the "Rackets Ship". In 1947-48 it was almost impossible to get nylon stockings. So the enterprising crew devised clever ruses to get by customs. So thousands of pretty limbs were sheathed in nylons, thanks to

"QUEEN MARY"

"For the period of her voyage she must be a whole way of life for her passengers. She must provide them with an experience that will somehow be different and better than a comparable experience they could have anywhere else. This experience must be one they will enjoy while they have it . . . and one they will never forget as long as they live".

Donald Wilson, former Chief Engineer of the "Queen." Mr. Wilson personifies the type of marine officers the Cunard Steamship Company is justly famous for.

The "QUEEN" is Welcomed by the City of Long Beach

Captain Treasure Jones on his bridge keeps an eye on the hundred's of yachts in the "Queen's" way.

Crew wave from the Queen Mary's proud forecastle.

The gaiety of the farewell party will be long remembered.

Every craft that could, flocked around this giant of oceanliners.

A majestic silhouette graces the outer harbor breakwater. The end of one career, the beginning of a new one.

Small boat escort leads the "Queen" up the California coast on her final voyage. The "Queen" had a distinguished passenger list, including many Long Beach officials.

View from the bridge as the Queen Mary reaches the outer harbor breakwater.

There was an armada of all types of craft to welcome the "stateliest ship in being."

Coast Guard, private craft of every description plus the Goodyear blimp, greet our famous "Queen" in 1967.

The "Queen" carried a record number of passengers (2,332) in August 1939. These were mostly U.S. citizens hurrying home, leaving Europe as W.W. II threatened.

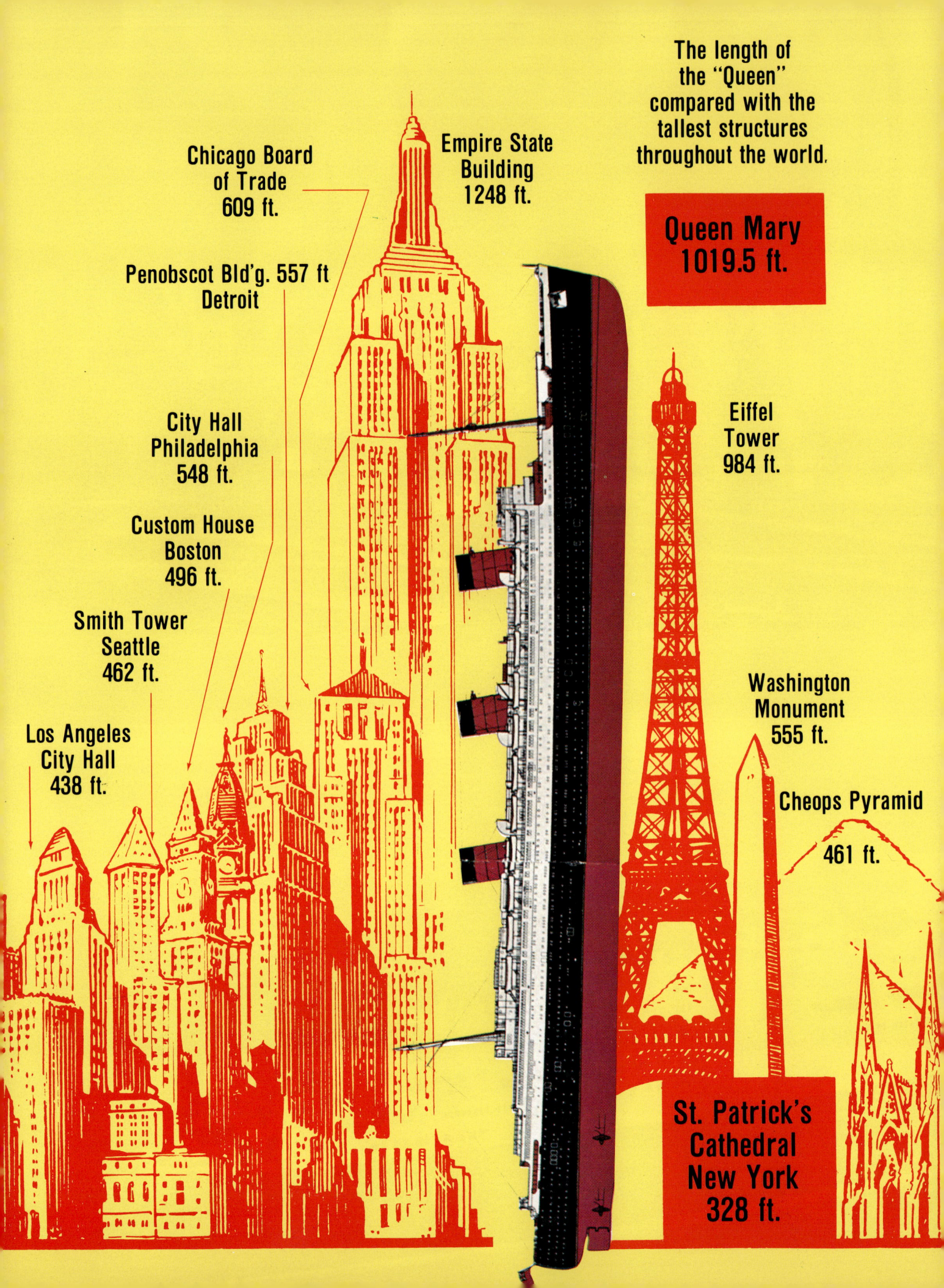

The length of the "Queen" compared with the tallest structures throughout the world.

Queen Mary 1019.5 ft.

Empire State Building 1248 ft.

Chicago Board of Trade 609 ft.

Penobscot Bld'g. 557 ft Detroit

City Hall Philadelphia 548 ft.

Custom House Boston 496 ft.

Smith Tower Seattle 462 ft.

Los Angeles City Hall 438 ft.

Eiffel Tower 984 ft.

Washington Monument 555 ft.

Cheops Pyramid 461 ft.

St. Patrick's Cathedral New York 328 ft.

Roll on, thou deep and dark blue Ocean,—
   roll!
Ten thousand fleets sweep over thee in
   vain;
Man marks the earth with ruin,—his
   control
Stops with the shore.

                LORD BYRON

A Progress List of The
WORLDS LARGEST LINERS

	GROSS TONNAGE	NAME	LENGTH IN FEET	DATES
	18,914	GREAT EASTERN	692	1858-1888
	20,904	CELTIC	700	1901-1928
	31,550	LUSITANIA	790	1907-1915
	30,696	MAURETANIA	790	1907-1935
	46,328	TITANIC	892	1912-1912
	52,022	BERENGARIA	919	1913-1938
	54,282	LEVIATHAN	950	1914-1938
	44,356	ILE DE FRANCE	793	1927-1959
	56,621	MAJESTIC	954	1922-1939
	79,280	NORMANDIE	1027	1935-1942
WORLD'S MOST FAMOUS	81,237	QUEEN MARY	1019	1936-
WORLD'S LARGEST	83,673	QUEEN ELIZABETH	1031	1940-1972
WORLD'S FASTEST	51,987	UNITED STATES	990	1952-
WORLD'S LONGEST	70,202	FRANCE (renamed NORWAY)	1035	1961-
WORLD'S NEWEST SUPERLINER	67,140	QUEEN ELIZABETH II	963	1969-

In the course of her long and honorable career the "MARY" carried many illustrious passengers, many world famous personalities. All held her in deep affection and respect. On her final cruise from England via Cape Horn, the atmosphere was one of gaiety, certainly, but also of reverence, and of nostalgia at the passing of an era of leisure and elegance.

STOP! An Illustrious Past and Entertaining Future for Generations to Come.